Navigating CARES Act Tax Credits: ERC and 1099 Self-Employed Tax Credit

A Comprehensive Guide to Maximizing COVID-19 Relief for Businesses and Self-Employed Individuals

Forbes Management Services
Decatur, Georgia
678-518-0688
https://forbesmgt.com/

FORBES
Management

Table Of Content

Chapter 1-Understanding The Difference Between The ERC and The Self-Employed Tax Credit

Understanding the ERC (Employee Retention Credit) and Self-Employed Tax Credit is crucial. ERC benefits employers, while the Self-Employed Tax Credit aids self-employed individuals. ERC focuses on retaining employees during COVID-19, while the Self-Employed Tax Credit supports freelancers with income loss. Both provide financial relief but differ in eligibility and application.

Chapter 2- Introduction to the 1099 Self-Employed Tax Credit

The 1099 Self-Employed Tax Credit was created as part of the Coronavirus Aid, Relief, and Economic Security (CARES) Act in 2020 to provide financial relief to self-employed individuals during the COVID-19 pandemic. This tax credit aims to make up for lost income for those who work for themselves, such as independent contractors, freelancers, gig workers, and sole proprietors.

Chapter 3 - Am I Eligible for the 1099 Self-Employed Tax Credit?

The most important first step is understanding if you are eligible for the 1099 Tax Credit...

Chapter 4 - How the 1099 Tax Credit Amount is Calculated

Once eligibility is confirmed, calculating how much credit you can claim is key. Here is a step-by-step walkthrough of how the credit calculations work...

Chapter 5 - Claiming the 1099 Credit on Your Tax Return

With your eligibility confirmed and credit amount calculated, now we turn to the actual tax filing process. We'll outline the

forms needed, key documentation, and exactly where to claim the credit come tax time...

Chapter 6 - Common Mistakes to Avoid When Claiming the 1099 Tax Credit

While powerful, this credit does come with complexity. We'll outline the most common errors filers make so you can avoid delays or issues come tax time...

Chapter 7 - Advanced Strategies to Maximize Your 1099 Tax Credit

Beyond just the basics, we'll explore pro tips and advanced strategies those savvy with taxes can use to unlock even more savings from this credit...

Chapter 8 - What to Expect in the Future with the 1099 Tax Credit

Finally, we end our guide looking at what is on the horizon for this credit, particularly with the potential for extension or expansion under proposed legislation...

Chapter 9 - Working with a Team of Experts: Maximizing Benefits with Lifetime Advisors and Forbes Insurance Services

Conclusion & Summary

In this comprehensive guide, you received everything you need to take full advantage of the 1099 Self-Employed Tax Credit from the CARES Act. We covered eligibility, calculations, claims processes, pitfalls to avoid, maximization strategies and what the future holds across 8 in-depth chapters. You are now armed with the insights needed to put this credit to work saving potentially thousands come tax time!

Chapter 1 - Understanding the Difference Between ERC and Self-Employed Tax Credits Under the CARES Act

In the wake of the COVID-19 pandemic, the U.S. government implemented various relief measures to support individuals and businesses facing financial challenges. Two significant tax credits introduced under the Coronavirus Aid, Relief, and Economic Security (CARES) Act were the Employee Retention Credit (ERC) and the Self-Employed Tax Credit. These credits aimed to provide financial assistance during the economic turmoil caused by the pandemic. While both credits serve a similar purpose, they are fundamentally different in their eligibility criteria, application, and who can benefit from them. In this chapter, we will explore the key distinctions between these two important CARES Act tax credits.

1. Nature of Beneficiaries

ERC (Employee Retention Credit): The ERC is primarily designed to benefit employers, including businesses of all sizes and tax-exempt organizations that have employees on their payroll. It is intended to incentivize employers to retain their workforce during periods of economic hardship by providing them with a tax credit.

Self-Employed Tax Credit: In contrast, the Self-Employed Tax Credit is aimed at providing relief to self-employed individuals, freelancers, gig workers, and sole proprietors who do not have employees on their payroll. It is specifically tailored for those who earn income through self-employment, where they are both the employer and employee.

2. Eligibility Criteria

ERC (Employee Retention Credit): To qualify for the ERC, employers must meet certain criteria, including experiencing a significant decline in gross receipts or being subject to a government-mandated shutdown or suspension of operations. Employers with employees who are unable to work due to COVID-19-related reasons may also be eligible. This credit is mainly tied to the employer's ability to retain employees during the pandemic.

Self-Employed Tax Credit: Eligibility for the Self-Employed Tax Credit is based on different criteria. Self-employed individuals must have experienced a reduction in their self-employment income during the tax year compared to prior years due to the pandemic. It is essential to have a Form 1099-NEC and be self-employed as an independent contractor or sole proprietor to qualify.

3. Application Process

ERC (Employee Retention Credit): Employers can claim the ERC by filing specific forms with the Internal Revenue Service (IRS), such as Form 941 for quarterly payroll tax returns. The credit is applied against the employer's portion of Social Security taxes and can be refunded if the credit exceeds the tax liability.

Self-Employed Tax Credit: Self-employed individuals can claim the Self-Employed Tax Credit on their individual tax returns, typically using Form 1040 or 1040-SR. This credit directly reduces their overall tax liability, including both income tax and self-employment tax.

4. Credit Amount Calculation

ERC (Employee Retention Credit): The ERC amount is calculated based on a percentage of qualified wages paid to eligible employees during the specified periods. The credit can cover up

to 50% of qualified wages, with a maximum credit amount per employee.

Self-Employed Tax Credit: The Self-Employed Tax Credit is calculated differently. It is determined by comparing the self-employed individual's net self-employment income for the current year (usually 2020, in the context of the CARES Act) to the prior year (2019). The credit percentage is based on the decline in income, and the maximum credit is applied against income tax.

5. Types of Expenses Covered

ERC (Employee Retention Credit): The ERC primarily covers qualified wages paid to employees. It includes both the wages paid to employees who continue to work, and wages paid to employees who are unable to work due to COVID-19-related reasons. Additionally, certain health plan expenses can be included.

Self-Employed Tax Credit: The Self-Employed Tax Credit is focused on the self-employment income of individuals. It considers the reduction in net self-employment income as the basis for calculating the credit. It does not cover expenses related to employees or payroll.

6. Impact on Employment

ERC (Employee Retention Credit): The ERC is intended to encourage employers to retain their employees, and it can help businesses maintain their workforce during challenging economic times. By providing a tax incentive, it aims to prevent layoffs and furloughs.

Self-Employed Tax Credit: The Self-Employed Tax Credit is geared towards self-employed individuals who may not have employees. It provides relief directly to those who rely on self-

employment income, such as freelancers and independent contractors, helping them cope with income reductions.

7. Duration

ERC (Employee Retention Credit): The ERC was initially introduced as part of the CARES Act in 2020 but has been extended and modified several times through subsequent legislation, including the Consolidated Appropriations Act, 2021, and the American Rescue Plan Act, 2021. The credit was extended until the end of 2021.

Self-Employed Tax Credit: The Self-Employed Tax Credit, on the other hand, is specific to the tax year 2020, as outlined in the CARES Act. It was designed as temporary relief for self-employed individuals impacted by the pandemic during that tax year.

In summary, while both the Employee Retention Credit (ERC) and the Self-Employed Tax Credit were introduced as part of the CARES Act to provide financial assistance during the COVID-19 pandemic, they differ significantly in their beneficiaries, eligibility criteria, application processes, and how the credit amounts are calculated. The ERC targets employers with employees on their payroll, while the Self-Employed Tax Credit is tailored for self-employed individuals. Understanding these distinctions is crucial for individuals and businesses to determine which credit is applicable to their specific circumstances and how they can benefit from the relief measures provided by the CARES Act.

Chapter 2 - Introduction to the 1099 Self-Employed Tax Credit

In the wake of the unprecedented COVID-19 pandemic that engulfed the world in 2020, governments scrambled to provide financial relief to those hit hardest by the economic fallout. Among the various measures implemented to mitigate the financial impact of the pandemic, the 1099 Self-Employed Tax Credit emerged as a vital lifeline for self-employed individuals in the United States. This chapter introduces you to the intricacies of the 1099 Self-Employed Tax Credit, shedding light on its origins, purpose, and the significant benefits it offers to freelancers, contractors, and others reliant on self-employment income.

The Genesis of the 1099 Self-Employed Tax Credit

The 1099 Self-Employed Tax Credit found its roots in the Coronavirus Aid, Relief and Economic Security (CARES) Act, a landmark piece of legislation enacted in March 2020. As the pandemic swept across the nation, it became evident that self-employed workers faced unique challenges. Unlike traditional employees, they lacked the safety nets of paid sick leave, unemployment benefits, and employer-sponsored healthcare. With clients cutting budgets, projects drying up, and businesses shuttering, many self-employed individuals found themselves in dire financial straits.

Recognizing the plight of these independent contractors, freelancers, gig workers, and sole proprietors, the U.S. government took action through the CARES Act. Within this comprehensive relief package, the 1099 Self-Employed Tax Credit was born. Its primary objective: to provide substantial

financial relief to those who rely on self-employment income and who had suffered income losses due to the pandemic.

The Essence of the 1099 Tax Credit

At its core, the 1099 Self-Employed Tax Credit operates as a mechanism to alleviate the tax burden on self-employed individuals. It accomplishes this by allowing them to reduce their 2020 tax liability based on the income losses they experienced in the preceding year. The stark reality for many self-employed individuals was a sudden and significant reduction in income, driven by factors such as:

- Economic Lockdowns: Businesses shuttered their doors, and lockdowns left many without clients or customers.
- Budget Constraints: Clients slashed budgets, leading to project cancellations or reductions in contracted work.
- Health Impacts: Small businesses, particularly those in sectors directly affected by the pandemic, faced health-related challenges that affected their ability to generate income.

The 1099 Tax Credit addresses these hardships by providing a dollar-for-dollar credit on tax returns, potentially covering up to 50% of the taxes owed on the individual's net self-employment income from the prior tax year. This practical application of the credit results in substantial savings come tax season, offering a critical lifeline when it's needed most.

Fostering Tax Compliance and Financial Resilience

One notable aspect of the 1099 Self-Employed Tax Credit is its role in promoting tax compliance among self-employed individuals. While the economic downturn presented immediate financial challenges, it also raised concerns about individuals skipping the filing of their tax returns due to reduced income.

However, the presence of this tax credit incentivized those impacted to continue filing their tax returns, even in the face of short-term financial difficulties.

This commitment to tax compliance not only ensures that self-employed workers fulfill their legal obligations but also positions them to benefit from the 1099 Tax Credit. By documenting their income and losses, they can unlock the financial relief this credit provides.

Navigating the Complexity

While the 1099 Self-Employed Tax Credit offers substantial benefits, it does not come without its complexities and challenges. Eligibility requirements are stringent, and correctly calculating the credit amount based on prior-year tax liabilities can be a daunting task. Moreover, the temporary nature of this credit imposes a time-sensitive element, requiring timely action to maximize its benefits.

This comprehensive guide aims to demystify the intricacies of the 1099 Self-Employed Tax Credit. In the chapters that follow, we will delve into every facet of this vital financial tool. From understanding the eligibility criteria to navigating the intricacies of tax forms and documentation, we will equip you with insider tips and best practices to ensure you make the most of this credit. Additionally, we'll highlight critical pitfalls to avoid, which could jeopardize your eligibility or reduce your credit amount.

Whether you are an independent contractor seeking to maximize your financial relief or someone who supports self-employed individuals, this guide serves as your roadmap to harnessing the power of the 1099 Self-Employed Tax Credit under the CARES Act. As we delve deeper into the details in the upcoming chapters, you'll gain the knowledge and confidence needed to navigate this essential resource effectively.

Chapter 3 - Determining Eligibility for the 1099 Self-Employed Tax Credit

The path to unlocking the benefits of the 1099 Self-Employed Tax Credit begins with understanding whether you meet the stringent eligibility criteria set forth by the Internal Revenue Service (IRS). In this chapter, we embark on a detailed exploration of these criteria, ascertaining whether you qualify for this valuable tax credit designed to alleviate the financial strain on self-employed individuals impacted by the COVID-19 pandemic.

Core Eligibility Criteria

Self-Employment Status

The foundational requirement for claiming the 1099 Tax Credit is self-employment. To be eligible, you must be self-employed as an independent contractor or a sole proprietor. This tax credit was specifically crafted to provide support to those who work for themselves and file a Form 1099-NEC. This includes a wide array of professionals, such as independent contractors, freelancers, gig workers, and sole proprietors who operate their own business entities.

It's essential to emphasize that you cannot be an employee of another company to qualify for this credit. The distinction between self-employment and traditional employment is a crucial one, as the IRS designed this credit with the unique challenges of self-employed individuals in mind.

Income Reduction Due to COVID-19

A significant prerequisite for eligibility is a verifiable reduction in self-employment income during the tax year 2020 compared to prior years. This reduction must be at least partially attributed

to the COVID-19 pandemic, which wreaked havoc on the global economy and led to widespread financial hardships.

The income reduction can manifest in various forms, including the loss of clients, decreased project opportunities, reduced working hours, or a decline in overall revenue. The IRS recognizes the pandemic's profound impact on self-employed individuals and has structured the credit to provide relief to those who experienced genuine financial setbacks.

Federal Tax Return Filing

To access the benefits of the 1099 Self-Employed Tax Credit during the 2020 tax year, you must fulfill an essential requirement: filing a federal tax return. Even if you would not typically be obligated to file a return based on your income level, filing becomes a necessity to reconcile this credit. It's a critical step to ensure you receive the financial relief you deserve.

Additional Eligibility Considerations

In addition to the core criteria, there are additional factors that can influence your eligibility for the 1099 Tax Credit:

Income Thresholds

The income thresholds serve as a determinant of the credit amount you can claim. To be eligible for the full credit amount, single filers must have earned under $20,000 during the tax year in question. For those married and filing jointly, the threshold rises to $40,000.

If your income exceeds these thresholds, you may still be eligible for partial credits on a sliding scale. The IRS has designed this system to provide some level of relief to a broader spectrum

of self-employed individuals, acknowledging that income variations exist within this group.

Health Insurance Requirements

Ensuring access to healthcare is of paramount importance, and the IRS has incorporated health insurance requirements as part of the eligibility criteria for the 1099 Self-Employed Tax Credit. To qualify, you must have maintained healthcare coverage for at least 50% of the tax year while self-employed.

This coverage can take various forms, including private insurance, a marketplace plan, or coverage through government programs like Medicare or Medicaid. The emphasis on healthcare coverage underscores the importance of safeguarding your well-being while pursuing self-employment opportunities.

In Summary

In summary, eligibility for the 1099 Self-Employed Tax Credit hinges on several key factors:

Your self-employment status as an independent contractor, freelancer, gig worker, or sole proprietor.

A demonstrable reduction in self-employment income in 2020 due, at least in part, to the impacts of the COVID-19 pandemic.

The filing of a federal tax return for the relevant tax year, even if not typically required.

Furthermore, you must consider income thresholds and health insurance coverage requirements. Earning below the specified income thresholds is essential for claiming the full credit amount, but partial credits are available for those with higher incomes. Maintaining healthcare coverage for at least half of the tax year is also crucial to meet the eligibility criteria.

Understanding and satisfying these eligibility requirements is the foundation upon which you can build your claim for the substantial tax relief provided by the 1099 Tax Credit. As we delve deeper into the subsequent chapters, you'll gain the knowledge and tools needed to navigate the application process with confidence, ensuring that you receive the financial support you deserve.

Chapter 4 - Calculating Your 1099 Tax Credit Amount: A Comprehensive Guide

Now that we've established your eligibility for the 1099 Self-Employed Tax Credit, it's time to delve into the crucial process of determining the actual credit amount you can claim. Calculating the credit amount involves meticulous tracking of your prior year's tax liability to serve as a benchmark, and then evaluating your 2020 reduction in self-employment income. In this chapter, we'll provide you with a step-by-step walkthrough of this essential process, demystifying the calculations and ensuring you can maximize your credit to its fullest potential.

Step 1: Determining Your 2019 Net Self-Employment Earnings

The journey toward calculating your 1099 Tax Credit begins with establishing a benchmark. This benchmark is your net self-employment earnings for the tax year 2019. To determine this figure accurately, follow these steps:

Gather all your income-related documents, including your 1099 forms and any other records of self-employment income.

If you are a sole proprietor, refer to your Schedule C profit and loss statement from your 2019 tax return. This document provides a comprehensive breakdown of your self-employment earnings and expenses.

Add up all your income from self-employment for 2019. This sum represents your net self-employment earnings for the benchmark year.

Step 2: Calculating the Tax Liability on Your 2019 Earnings

With your 2019 net self-employment earnings established, the next crucial step is to calculate the tax liability associated with those earnings. To do this, follow these steps:

Based on your total earnings amount for 2019, determine the total tax liability you incurred for those self-employment profits.

Consult your 2019 Form 1040 Schedule 2, specifically looking at line 57. This line item provides you with the specific tax liability amount associated with your self-employment earnings for that year.

Step 3: Documenting Your 2020 Net Self-Employment Earnings

Having successfully determined your tax liability for 2019, you will now need to calculate your net self-employment earnings for the tax year 2020. Follow the same methodology as before, gathering all relevant income-related documents and utilizing your Schedule C profit and loss statement if you are a sole proprietor. However, be prepared for the likelihood that your 2020 earnings will be lower, given the impact of the COVID-19 pandemic on many self-employed individuals.

Step 4: Subtracting 2020 Earnings from 2019 Earnings

Now that you have established your earnings for both 2019 and 2020, calculate the difference between the two figures. This difference represents your decline in self-employment income for the year 2020. It's this income loss that forms the foundation for your tax credit calculation.

Step 5: Determining the Tax Credit Percentage Based on Income Decline

Your next step is to determine the tax credit percentage based on the income decline you identified in step 4. To calculate this percentage, follow this formula:

Divide your income loss in 2020 by your net earnings amount from 2019. This division yields a percentage that signifies the extent to which your self-employment income decreased from one year to the next.

This percentage is a crucial factor in determining the final tax credit amount you can claim.

Step 6: Multiplying the Credit Percentage by Your 2019 Liability

With the tax credit percentage established, you are now ready to calculate the actual 1099 Tax Credit amount you can claim. Follow these steps:

Multiply the tax credit percentage you determined in step 5 by your 2019 tax liability amount (the figure you found on line 57 of your 2019 Form 1040 Schedule 2).

This final calculation provides you with the precise total 1099 Tax Credit amount that you are eligible to claim on your 2020 tax return.

By completing this comprehensive 6-step process using your real-world financial figures, you gain clarity on the exact credit figure to include directly on your 2020 taxes. This amount represents the financial relief and support designed to alleviate the impact of income reductions caused by the COVID-19 pandemic.

It's important to note that the calculations can be intricate, and individual circumstances may vary. Therefore, it's advisable to consult with a tax professional or use tax preparation software to ensure accuracy in determining your 1099 Tax Credit amount. This meticulous approach ensures that you maximize the relief available to you, providing valuable financial assistance during these challenging times.

As we progress through the subsequent chapters, you will further enhance your understanding of how to claim this credit and avoid common pitfalls that can potentially diminish your eligibility or credit amount.

Chapter 5 - Claiming Your 1099 Tax Credit on Your Tax Return: A Step-by-Step Guide

Now that you've determined your eligibility and meticulously calculated the amount of the 1099 Self-Employed Tax Credit you are entitled to, it's time to embark on the process of claiming this valuable tax credit and realizing the savings it offers. Fortunately, the steps for claiming the credit are straightforward, and in this chapter, we will guide you through each crucial element of the process.

Step 1: Fill Out and File IRS Form 1040 or 1040-SR

The initial step in claiming the 1099 Tax Credit involves filling out and filing your federal income tax return. To successfully claim this credit, you must complete either the standard Form 1040 or the 1040-SR if you are a senior taxpayer. It's important to note that filing a tax return is an essential requirement, even if your income falls below the standard filing thresholds for the tax year 2020.

Filing your tax return is not only a legal obligation but also a critical step to qualify for the credit. These forms serve as the primary documentation for your financial activities during the tax year and are essential for reconciling your tax liability and claiming the credit accurately.

Step 2: Attach Schedule C Documenting Income Sources (For Sole Proprietors)

If you operate as a sole proprietor, this step is particularly crucial. You must include a completed Schedule C along with your tax return. Schedule C serves as a comprehensive record of

your self-employment income sources and provides a detailed breakdown of your net profit or loss from your own business.

The inclusion of Schedule C is essential for substantiating the sharp decline in your net earnings, a decline attributed to the impact of the COVID-19 pandemic. This schedule provides the IRS with a clear and comprehensive view of your self-employment activities and financial status during the tax year, thereby validating your eligibility for the 1099 Tax Credit.

Step 3: Complete Form 8995

Form 8995, titled "Qualified Business Income Deduction Simplified Computation," is a specialized IRS form specifically designed for calculating and claiming the 1099 Tax Credit amount. Beyond its role as a calculation tool, Form 8995 also serves as additional documentation that verifies your eligibility criteria for the credit during the tax year 2020.

Completing Form 8995 accurately is paramount, as it directly impacts the credit amount you can claim. This form is tailored to the unique circumstances of self-employed individuals who have experienced income reductions due to the COVID-19 pandemic. It streamlines the process of calculating your tax credit, ensuring that you can access the relief you deserve.

Step 4: Claim the Credit Amount on Form 1040

In the final step of claiming the 1099 Tax Credit, you'll need to transfer the final tax credit figure from Form 8995 directly onto your Form 1040 or 1040-SR. This is the step where you officially claim the credit, reducing your total tax liability to the IRS for the tax year 2020.

It's important to note that there is a designated section on these tax forms for claiming COVID-19-related credits from the CARES Act legislation. Be sure to locate and complete this section

accurately, as it ensures that your credit is properly attributed to the relief efforts aimed at self-employed individuals impacted by the pandemic.

Ensuring Your Documents Are Complete

With Form 1040 or 1040-SR, Schedule C (for sole proprietors), Form 8995, and your attached 1099-NEC or NECs (for independent contractors), you have assembled all the necessary documents and information required to substantiate and unlock the 1099 Tax Credit come tax time. These four components contain the essential details and calculations that enable you to save substantially on your tax liability.

However, it's worth emphasizing that while the process is straightforward, meticulous attention to detail is crucial. Accurate completion of these forms ensures that you maximize the financial relief offered by the 1099 Tax Credit, providing critical support during these challenging times.

As we continue to navigate the complexities of tax regulations and credits, remember that seeking professional guidance from a tax advisor or using reputable tax preparation software can provide additional assurance that your claims are accurate and optimized. These resources can help you navigate the nuances of tax law, safeguard your eligibility for the credit, and ensure that you receive the maximum savings available to you.

In the chapters ahead, we will delve deeper into the specific details of the 1099 Self-Employed Tax Credit, addressing common pitfalls to avoid and advanced strategies to maximize your tax relief. By mastering these key elements of the process, you'll be well-equipped to make the most of this vital financial resource.

Chapter 6 - Common Pitfalls to Avoid When Claiming the 1099 Tax Credit: Maximizing Your Eligibility and Payout

While the 1099 Tax Credit offers a crucial lifeline to self-employed individuals impacted by the COVID-19 pandemic, it's essential to navigate the claims process with precision. Even seemingly minor mistakes can jeopardize your eligibility for the credit or reduce the amount you're entitled to. Most of these issues stem from a misunderstanding of the temporary nature of this credit under the CARES Act legislation. In this chapter, we'll explore the most common pitfalls to steer clear of to ensure you receive the full benefits you deserve.

Pitfall 1: Claiming Too Late

One of the fundamental aspects to grasp about the 1099 Tax Credit is its time-sensitive nature. It applies exclusively to the 2020 tax year filings, which must be completed in the year 2021. Any attempts to claim the credit through amended returns or filings outside this narrow 12-month window are deemed ineligible.

It's critical to recognize that this credit is not a permanent fixture of the tax code. Failing to act within the prescribed timeframe can result in the forfeiture of financial relief that could significantly ease your financial hardships. To maximize your eligibility for the credit, ensure that you adhere to the designated filing period and meet all the necessary deadlines.

Pitfall 2: Insufficient Healthcare Coverage

Meeting the healthcare coverage requirements is a pivotal aspect of claiming the 1099 Tax Credit. To qualify, you must have

maintained healthcare coverage for at least 50% of the tax year while self-employed. This includes private insurance, coverage through a marketplace plan, or healthcare provided by Medicare or Medicaid.

One common mistake that can jeopardize your claim is failing to meet the healthcare coverage threshold. Gaps or dropped plans that result in less than 50% coverage throughout the tax year can disqualify your entire claim. It's imperative to maintain adequate healthcare coverage to safeguard your eligibility for the credit.

Pitfall 3: Rounded Income Figures

Precision in reporting your income is paramount when calculating the 1099 Tax Credit amount. Every dollar matters, and even slight discrepancies can lead to faulty calculations that may reduce the amount of the credit you are entitled to or trigger IRS notice letters.

To ensure accuracy, avoid rounding income figures or providing estimates. Instead, use exact figures derived from your financial records, including your 1099 forms and Schedule C profit/loss statements. By maintaining precise records and calculations, you can maximize the credit amount you claim and reduce the risk of complications with the IRS.

Pitfall 4: Using Wrong Years for Income Comparisons

When determining your eligibility for the 1099 Tax Credit, it's crucial to make accurate income comparisons. Your 2020 decline in income should be assessed in relation to the prior tax year of 2019—not any other period. Using inconsistent years for comparison can result in faulty credit rate calculations and potential discrepancies in your claim.

To avoid this pitfall, ensure that you correctly align your income data with the relevant tax years. A consistent and accurate approach to income comparisons will help you claim the credit with confidence and precision.

Pitfall 5: Trying to "Double Dip" on Multiple Business Relief Credits

While it's possible to qualify for multiple relief programs under the CARES Act, the credits themselves have built-in safeguards against claiming overlapping benefits. Attempting to "double dip" by claiming multiple credits for the same expenses or income reductions can lead to complications and potential penalties.

To navigate this pitfall, carefully evaluate which relief program best suits your circumstances and select the optimal one. By adhering to the guidelines and restrictions associated with each credit, you can ensure that you receive the maximum benefits without inadvertently running afoul of the rules.

Pitfall 6: Submitting Unsupported Tax Documentation

The 1099 Tax Credit requires thorough substantiation, including filed tax returns and 1099 forms from prior years. Failing to provide adequate supporting documentation can trigger automatic denial of your claim and may lead to IRS audits or inquiries.

To avoid this pitfall, maintain meticulous records of your financial activities, including copies of filed tax returns and all relevant 1099 forms. By keeping comprehensive records and providing the necessary documentation, you can fortify your claim and enhance your eligibility for the credit.

Pitfall 7: Waiting on Backlogs for Amended Returns

Correcting errors or adjusting your tax filings is a standard practice, but it's important to be mindful of the timelines associated with amended returns. For the 1099 Tax Credit, it's advisable to address any mistakes or modifications in the following tax year, such as during your 2021 filings.

Attempting to amend returns for the tax years 2019 or 2020 outside the normal non-pandemic 12-month window can lead to complications and potential delays in receiving the credit. To streamline the process and ensure timely resolution, focus on making necessary corrections in the current tax year rather than relying on amendments for prior years.

Navigating Pitfalls for Maximum Benefit

These common pitfalls are worth heeding as you navigate the process of claiming the 1099 Tax Credit. By avoiding these pitfalls and adhering to the prescribed guidelines, you can maximize your benefits from this temporary credit, easing the financial hardships caused by the COVID-19 pandemic.

Vigilant and precise filing is the key to justifiably maximizing the benefits offered by the 1099 Tax Credit. While the credit is time-sensitive and comes with specific eligibility criteria, careful attention to detail and compliance with the rules can ensure that you receive the financial relief you need. In the following chapters, we will delve into advanced strategies for optimizing your credit, as well as explore what the future may hold for this vital relief program.

Chapter 7 - Advanced Strategies to Maximize Your 1099 Tax Credit: Pro Tips and Insider Techniques

While the 1099 Tax Credit offers substantial relief to self-employed individuals impacted by the COVID-19 pandemic, there are advanced strategies that savvy taxpayers can employ to extract even greater value from this CARES Act program. These insider techniques can help you maximize your savings and optimize the benefits you receive. In this chapter, we will explore these advanced strategies to ensure you're making the most of the 1099 Tax Credit.

Strategy 1: Shift Business Expenses Into Other Years

One effective way to increase your 1099 Tax Credit is to strategically shift business expenses into different tax years. Since a lower net income in 2020 leads to a higher credit, pulling deductible expenses from 2020 into 2019 or deferring them until 2021 can help minimize your profits on paper for the 2020 tax year.

For example, if you have the flexibility to delay certain deductible expenses until the following tax year, you can reduce your taxable income in 2020, potentially increasing the credit amount you qualify for. However, it's crucial to consult with a tax professional or financial advisor to ensure that this strategy aligns with your overall financial goals and business plan.

Strategy 2: Split Business Efforts Across Multiple Entities

If you launched new businesses in 2020 or plan to do so in the future, consider housing income streams in separate legal entities. By structuring your businesses in this way, you can claim 1099 Tax Credits against established businesses while allowing new ventures to scale independently.

This strategy can be particularly advantageous if you anticipate varying levels of income and profitability across your business entities. Careful structuring can help you optimize the allocation of credits to the entities that need them most, ultimately maximizing your overall savings.

Strategy 3: Reinvest Credit Savings Back Into Your Business

Rather than simply pocketing the tax savings from the 1099 Tax Credit, consider reinvesting these funds back into your business. This can fuel growth by allocating the credits toward marketing initiatives, acquiring new equipment, or addressing any capacity shortfalls exposed by the pandemic.

Reinvesting in your business not only stimulates growth but also positions your enterprise for long-term success. By strategically allocating the tax savings, you can enhance your business's resilience and competitiveness in the post-pandemic landscape.

Strategy 4: Review Insurance Policy Premiums

To further reduce your net earnings and maximize your 1099 Tax Credit, consider reviewing your insurance policy premiums. Boosting health insurance premiums above 50% of your gross annual income can effectively lower your net earnings, making you eligible for a larger credit.

While increasing your health insurance premiums may come with incremental policy costs, the savings derived from the 1099 Tax Credit can often exceed these additional expenses. However,

it's essential to strike a balance and avoid overspending on premiums, especially if your income is expected to rise in subsequent years.

Strategy 5: Develop Contingency Plans for Future Downturns

The lessons learned from the challenges of 2020 can be instrumental in preparing for future economic downturns. To safeguard your financial stability and eligibility for the 1099 Tax Credit, consider developing contingency plans that allow you to quickly reduce expenses in response to demand drops.

Whether you establish a rainy-day fund or implement procedures to pause non-essential spending, having plans in place can help you navigate future uncertainties with greater ease. These contingency plans can also contribute to lower net earnings, potentially increasing your credit amount.

Strategy 6: Consider 2023 Tax Impacts When Making 2022 Moves

While the 1099 Tax Credit provides immediate relief, it's crucial to consider its potential long-term implications on your tax situation. Income spikes in 2022, especially for those who are actively rebuilding from the pandemic, could lead to higher tax bills in 2023 after the credits expire.

To strategically manage your tax liability, assess the impact of your 2022 growth plans on your future tax obligations. Consult with a tax professional to develop a comprehensive tax strategy that considers both immediate and future tax considerations.

Maximizing the Benefits of the 1099 Tax Credit

While these advanced strategies are not exhaustive, they offer valuable insights into how you can extend the power of the

1099 Tax Credit in both the short and long-term. By implementing these techniques, you can make the most of this temporary relief program and ensure that you're not leaving any savings on the table.

It's important to note that the effectiveness of these strategies may vary depending on your unique financial circumstances and business goals. Therefore, it's advisable to consult with a qualified tax advisor or financial expert who can provide personalized guidance tailored to your specific situation.

By combining your knowledge of the 1099 tax credit with these advanced strategies, you can optimize your eligibility, maximize your savings, and navigate the complexities of the tax code with confidence. In the following chapter, we will explore what the future holds for the 1099 Tax Credit and provide insights into potential developments on the horizon.

Chapter 8 - What to Expect in the Future with the 1099 Tax Credit: Navigating Uncertainty

As a product of COVID relief legislation, the future of the 1099 Tax Credit remains shrouded in uncertainty. While tax codes are subject to change and adaptation, as of now, this credit stands as a one-time stimulus measure specifically designed for the 2020 tax year filings. However, historical precedents during times of crisis and economic turbulence can provide insights into potential developments on the horizon.

Possibility 1: Extension or Expansion in New Legislation

The ongoing and persistent impact of the COVID-19 pandemic throughout 2021 may prompt lawmakers to consider extending the 1099 Tax Credit beyond its initial scope. It's not unprecedented for similar measures to be extended or expanded during times of economic hardship. For instance, during the recession of 2008-2009, various economic stimulus measures were extended and broadened to provide ongoing support to affected individuals and businesses.

In the current economic climate, where self-employed individuals continue to face challenges and income disruptions, there is a possibility that legislators may revisit and expand the 1099 Tax Credit in new legislation. This could extend its availability to 2021 tax filings or make it more accessible to a broader range of self-employed workers.

Possibility 2: Permanent Establishment of Related Self-Employed Credits

Another potential future development could involve the establishment of a new, permanent tax credit tailored specifically for self-employed workers. This credit could emerge as part of broader tax overhaul proposals, aimed at providing ongoing support to the self-employed community.

One such proposal that aligns with the goals of the current temporary credit is a simplified 30% deduction for all health insurance costs incurred by self-employed filers. This permanent deduction could replace or complement the 1099 Tax Credit, offering long-term financial relief to self-employed individuals who bear the burden of health insurance costs.

Possibility 3: Sunsetting Without Further Action

In the absence of executive or legislative action, the 1099 Tax Credit will naturally expire, leaving it unused for those who did not leverage it in their 2020 tax filings. This would result in taxpayers missing out on potential financial relief just as economic conditions may start to stabilize and contracts begin flowing again.

This scenario underscores the importance of acting promptly to claim the credit if you are eligible. By taking advantage of the 1099 Tax Credit in your 2020 tax filings, you can secure immediate savings and financial assistance. Delaying the process could mean missing out on a valuable resource designed to alleviate the financial strain caused by the pandemic.

Staying Informed and Prepared

While short-term uncertainty prevails in 2021, the long-term trend toward supporting self-employed taxpayers and gig

workers appears to be gaining bipartisan support, based on past measures. However, for individuals seeking immediate relief, the only guaranteed option for realizing savings is by leveraging the 1099 Tax Credit in their 2020 tax filings.

To stay informed about potential developments and changes to tax legislation, it's essential to monitor proposals in Congress and remain engaged in discussions related to self-employed tax benefits. Additionally, consulting with a tax professional or financial advisor can provide you with personalized guidance as the year unfolds. These experts can help you navigate the ever-changing landscape of tax laws and ensure that you are making the most of available credits and deductions.

In summary, while the future of the 1099 Tax Credit remains uncertain, the importance of taking action in the present is clear. By capitalizing on this credit in your 2020 tax filings, you can secure tangible and immediate financial relief. Stay vigilant, stay informed, and be prepared to act on the opportunities that arise, whether through the extension of existing credits or the establishment of new, permanent solutions. In the world of taxes, proactive measures often yield the most beneficial results.

Chapter 9 - Working with a Team of Experts: Maximizing Benefits with Lifetime Advisors and Forbes Insurance Services

In the realm of financial planning, especially when navigating the intricacies of tax credits and financial protection during a crisis, having a team of experts by your side can make all the difference. Lifetime Advisors and Forbes Insurance Services are two companies that have come together to provide clients with a comprehensive suite of services, including support for the Employee Retention Credit (ERC) and the Self-Employed Tax Credit, both of which were introduced under the CARES Act. This chapter delves into the advantages of working with such expert teams and how they can help you secure your financial future.

Lifetime Advisors: Your Partner in Financial Planning Our Diverse Team of Planning Professionals

Lifetime Advisors is a company comprised of a diverse team of planning professionals, each with decades of experience in their individual fields. They have joined forces to address a gap in the market that has often left individuals and businesses underserved or unable to access the support they need from larger accounting firms. This team of experts includes financial planners, tax advisors, and consultants who are well-versed in the complexities of financial planning and tax strategies.

Providing Peace of Mind

One of the primary objectives of Lifetime Advisors is to empower their clients to focus on what they do best — whether that's running a business or pursuing their passions — while ensuring that they are adequately positioned and protected from unintentional over taxation. The Internal Revenue Code offers numerous incentives for business owners, but navigating these complexities can be a daunting task. Lifetime Advisors steps in to provide the necessary guidance and expertise to help clients make the most of these opportunities.

The Role of Lifetime Advisors in the Self-Employed Tax Credit

The Self-Employed Tax Credit, introduced under the CARES Act, is a crucial lifeline for self-employed individuals who experienced income reductions due to the pandemic. Lifetime Advisors plays a pivotal role in assisting clients in maximizing this credit. They work closely with self-employed individuals, freelancers, and independent contractors to ensure that they meet the eligibility criteria and properly calculate the credit amount. By leveraging their expertise, clients can confidently claim the credit and reduce their overall tax liability.

Forbes Insurance Services: ERC and Self-Employed Tax Credit Specialists

A Brief Overview of Forbes Insurance Services

Forbes Insurance Services specializes in helping individuals and businesses navigate the complexities of the Employee Retention Credit (ERC) and the Self-Employed Tax Credit. These credits were introduced in response to the economic challenges posed by the COVID-19 pandemic, with a focus on providing financial relief to employers and self-employed individuals.

Understanding the ERC

The Employee Retention Credit (ERC) was initially targeted at W-2 employers to mitigate the economic impact of the pandemic. However, Forbes Insurance Services recognized the importance of expanding access to these credits to self-employed individuals and gig workers. They played a significant role in advocating for the expansion of the CARES Act to include these groups.

ERC and Self-Employed Tax Credit Eligibility

Forbes Insurance Services helps individuals understand the eligibility criteria for both the ERC and the Self-Employed Tax Credit. The ERC eligibility is tied to factors such as significant declines in gross receipts or government-mandated shutdowns. On the other hand, the Self-Employed Tax Credit requires individuals to meet specific criteria related to self-employment income reductions due to COVID-19.

Navigating the Application Process

Applying for these tax credits can be a complex process, but Forbes Insurance Services simplifies it for clients. They assist individuals in completing the necessary forms and documentation to claim the ERC or the Self-Employed Tax Credit. Their expertise ensures that clients can access the financial relief they deserve.

The Role of Forbes Insurance Services in Supporting Self-Employed Individuals

For self-employed individuals who rely on their own businesses for income, the Self-Employed Tax Credit is a crucial lifeline. Forbes Insurance Services specializes in helping these individuals identify their eligibility, gather the required documents, and amend their tax returns as needed to claim the

credit. Their support extends to guiding clients through the entire process, from start to finish.

The Synergy of Expertise: Lifetime Advisors and Forbes Insurance Services

The collaboration between Lifetime Advisors and Forbes Insurance Services represents a powerful synergy of expertise. Both companies share a commitment to helping clients secure their financial futures and maximize the benefits available to them under the CARES Act.

Seamless Integration of Services

Working with both Lifetime Advisors and Forbes Insurance Services means that clients can benefit from a seamless integration of services. Lifetime Advisors offer comprehensive financial planning and tax strategies, while Forbes Insurance Services specialize in ERC and Self-Employed Tax Credit support. This holistic approach ensures that clients receive well-rounded guidance tailored to their unique circumstances.

Expert Guidance at Every Step

Whether you're a business owner seeking to understand the intricacies of the ERC or a self-employed individual looking to claim the Self-Employed Tax Credit, the expert teams at Lifetime Advisors and Forbes Insurance Services are with you at every step. They provide personalized guidance, answer your questions, and ensure that you make informed decisions that align with your financial goals.

Maximizing Financial Relief

The ultimate goal of both companies is to help clients maximize the financial relief available to them. Whether it's through strategic tax planning, claiming tax credits, or ensuring proper financial protection, clients can trust that they are in capable

hands. By working with a team of experts, individuals and businesses can secure their financial stability and peace of mind during challenging times.

In conclusion, the expertise of Lifetime Advisors and Forbes Insurance Services offers a valuable resource for individuals and businesses seeking to navigate the complexities of tax credits introduced under the CARES Act. With a commitment to providing comprehensive support, these companies empower their clients to make the most of available opportunities and secure their financial futures. Whether you're a business owner or a self-employed individual, having a dedicated team of experts by your side can make a significant difference in achieving your financial goals and ensuring financial peace of mind.

Conclusion: Navigating CARES Act Tax Credits for Financial Relief

In this comprehensive guide, we have embarked on a journey through the intricate landscape of the tax credits introduced under the Coronavirus Aid, Relief, and Economic Security (CARES) Act. These tax credits were designed to provide crucial financial relief to individuals and businesses grappling with the unprecedented challenges brought about by the COVID-19 pandemic. Our aim has been to equip you with the knowledge and insights needed to navigate these credits effectively, whether you are a business owner, an employee, or a self-employed individual.

Throughout the chapters of this book, we have explored two key tax credits that have played a pivotal role in offering economic support during these trying times:

1. **The Employee Retention Credit (ERC)**: Initially aimed at W-2 employers, this credit was expanded to include a broader range of businesses and organizations. We delved into the eligibility criteria, calculation methods, and the application process for the ERC. By understanding the nuances of this credit, employers were empowered to make informed decisions regarding employee retention, ultimately mitigating the economic impacts of the pandemic.

2. **The 1099 Self-Employed Tax Credit**: This credit was specifically crafted to provide relief to self-employed individuals, freelancers, and independent contractors who saw their incomes decline due to COVID-19. We examined the eligibility requirements, the process of calculating the credit amount, and the steps involved in

claiming it. By unraveling the complexities of this credit, self-employed individuals were able to secure the financial relief they needed to weather the storm.

In addition to the technical details of these tax credits, we also explored common pitfalls and challenges that individuals and businesses faced while navigating them. By highlighting these potential stumbling blocks, we aimed to help our readers steer clear of avoidable mistakes and complications.

Moreover, we delved into advanced strategies that could be employed to maximize the benefits of these tax credits. These strategies went beyond the basics, offering insights on how to optimize financial relief and plan for the future effectively.

In Chapter 9, we introduced you to two expert teams, Lifetime Advisors and Forbes Insurance Services, who specialize in guiding clients through the complexities of these tax credits. Their expertise and commitment to financial planning and protection have been invaluable assets for those seeking to secure their financial futures.

In our exploration of the future of these tax credits, we recognized the uncertainties that lie ahead. While the immediate future remains uncertain, the long-term trend of supporting individuals and businesses in times of economic turbulence seems poised to continue. We encouraged our readers to stay vigilant, monitor developments in Congress, and remain ready to take action when opportunities arise.

Summary: Navigating CARES Act Tax Credits for Financial Relief

The CARES Act Tax Credits have been instrumental in providing financial relief to individuals and businesses impacted by the COVID-19 pandemic. In this comprehensive guide, we have covered key aspects of two significant tax credits introduced under this legislation:

1. **The Employee Retention Credit (ERC)**: This credit was expanded to support a wide range of businesses, including those that experienced significant declines in gross receipts or were subject to government-mandated shutdowns. We explored eligibility criteria, calculation methods, and the application process.

2. **The 1099 Self-Employed Tax Credit**: Tailored for self-employed individuals, freelancers, and independent contractors, this credit addressed income reductions resulting from the pandemic. We provided insights into eligibility requirements, credit calculation, and claiming procedures.

Throughout the guide, we emphasized the importance of understanding eligibility criteria, avoiding common pitfalls, and implementing advanced strategies to maximize benefits. We introduced expert teams, Lifetime Advisors and Forbes Insurance Services, who specialize in guiding clients through these credits.

As we looked toward the future, we acknowledged the uncertainties surrounding the continuation of these credits. While the immediate outlook remained uncertain, bipartisan support for measures benefiting individuals and businesses during economic crises suggested a potential for further support.

In conclusion, this guide has been a valuable resource for individuals and businesses seeking to navigate the intricacies of CARES Act Tax Credits. By empowering readers with knowledge, insights, and expert guidance, we aimed to assist them in securing financial relief, making informed decisions, and planning for a more stable and prosperous future. As we move forward, staying informed and prepared remains key to

leveraging available opportunities for financial relief and
security.

Forbes Management Services LLC is an independent state of Georgia company, owned and operated by Yvonne M. Forbes (Forbes Management Services LLC) maintains a strategic alliance with Lifetime Advisors, LLC. Lifetime Advisors, LLC, is a state of Wisconsin marketing and consulting company offering products and services to business owners and high net worth individuals through its nationwide network of independent contractor Field Consultants. Forbes Management Services LLC as an independent contractor Field Consultant for Lifetime Advisors, LLC, refers clients to Lifetime Advisors, LLC for compensation. Though Lifetime Advisors, LLC compensates Forbes Management as an Independent Contractor, Forbes Management Services LLC is a separate company, independent from and not affiliated with Lifetime Advisors, LLC.

Lifetime Advisors, LLC is a consulting and marketing firm organized in Wisconsin. Neither Lifetime Advisors, LLC nor its affiliates or Field Consultants offer tax, legal or investment advice. Consult with your tax, legal or investment adviser before implementing any strategy that Lifetime Advisors, LLC suggests you consider.

For help getting started contact a Forbes Management Services expert.

Yvonne Forbes -Yvonne@ForbesMGT.com

Yurith Brownie -Yurith@ForbesMGT.com

Forbes Management Services
Decatur, Georgia
678-518-0688
https://forbesmgt.com/